Spot the Differences

Alligator or Crocodile?

by Adeline J. Zimmerman

Bullfrog Books

Ideas for Parents and Teachers

Bullfrog Books let children practice reading informational text at the earliest reading levels. Repetition, familiar words, and photo labels support early readers.

Before Reading

- Discuss the cover photo. What does it tell them?
- Look at the picture glossary together. Read and discuss the words.

Read the Book

- "Walk" through the book and look at the photos. Let the child ask questions. Point out the photo labels.
- Read the book to the child, or have him or her read independently.

After Reading

- Prompt the child to think more. Ask: Have you ever seen an alligator or crocodile? Would you like to? Why or why not?

Bullfrog Books are published by Jump!
5357 Penn Avenue South
Minneapolis, MN 55419
www.jumplibrary.com

Library of Congress Cataloging-in-Publication Data

Names: Zimmerman, Adeline J., author.
Title: Alligator or crocodile? / Adeline J. Zimmerman.
Description: Bullfrog books. | Minneapolis, MN Jump!, Inc., [2022]
Series: Spot the differences
Includes index. | Audience: Ages 5–8
Identifiers: LCCN 2021028387 (print)
LCCN 2021028388 (ebook)
ISBN 9781636903347 (hardcover)
ISBN 9781636903354 (paperback)
ISBN 9781636903361 (ebook)
Subjects: LCSH: Alligators—Juvenile literature.
Crocodiles—Juvenile literature.
Classification: LCC QL666.C925 Z56 2022 (print)
LCC QL666.C925 (ebook)
DDC 597.98/4—dc23
LC record available at https://lccn.loc.gov/2021028387
LC ebook record available at https://lccn.loc.gov/2021028388

Editor: Jenna Gleisner
Designer: Michelle Sonnek

Photo Credits: Eric Isselee/Shutterstock, cover (top), 1 (left), 24 (bottom); John Kasawa/Shutterstock, cover (bottom), 1 (right); Roberto La Rosa/Shutterstock, 4; worananphoto/Shutterstock, 5; Michael Schoonover/Shutterstock, 6–7 (top); Rudi Hulshof/Shutterstock, 6–7 (bottom); Shimon Bar/Shutterstock, 8–9; Steve Allen/Shutterstock, 10–11; SunflowerMomma/Shutterstock, 12–13, 23br; Sarah Camille/Shutterstock, 14–15, 23tr; Dennis W Donohue/Shutterstock, 16–17, 23tl; Michel VIARD/iStock, 18–19; reptiles4all/Shutterstock, 20; Photoongraphy/Shutterstock, 21; Deborah Ferrin/Shutterstock, 22 (left); Firepac/Shutterstock, 22 (right); iStock, 23bl; Ton Bangkeaw/Shutterstock, 24 (top).

Printed in the United States of America at Corporate Graphics in North Mankato, Minnesota.

Table of Contents

How to Use This Book

In this book, you will see pictures of both alligators and crocodiles. Can you tell which one is in each picture?

Hint: You can find the answers if you flip the book upside down!

Tails and Scales

This is an alligator.
We call it a gator.

This is a crocodile.
We call it a croc.

They look alike.

But they have differences.

Can you spot them?

Let's see!

snout

A gator's snout is wide.
It looks like a U.
A croc's looks like a V.
Which is this?

Answer: alligator

A croc's teeth always stick out.

A gator's don't.

Which is this?

Answer: crocodile

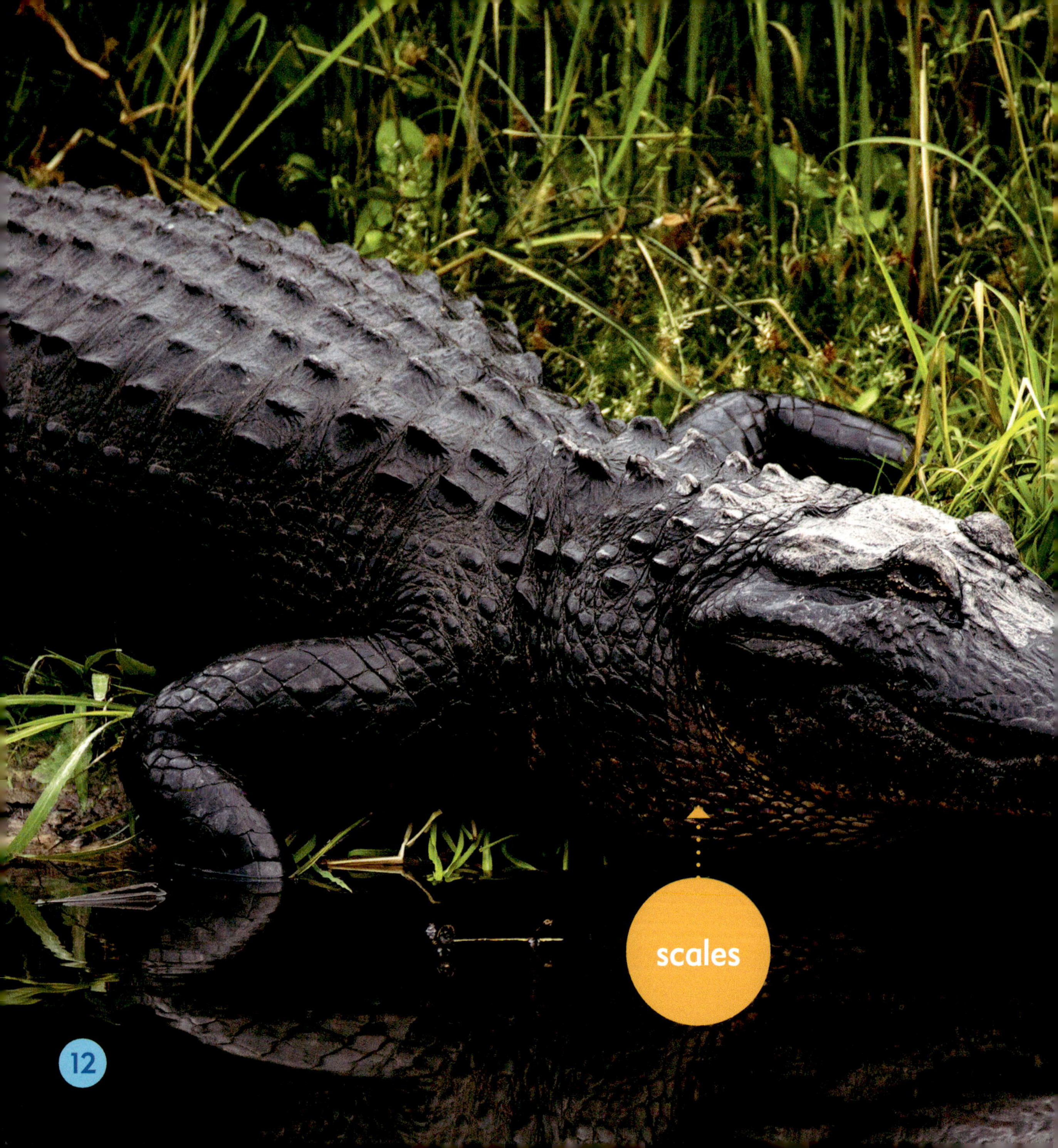
scales

A gator has dark scales.
A croc's are lighter.
Which is this?

Answer: alligator

Both have claws.
Crocs have fringe.
Gators don't.
Whose leg is this?

Answer: crocodile

claw

Gators live in fresh water.

Crocs live in salt water.

Look at this pond.

Who swims in it?

Answer: alligator

Both have babies.
They are small.
What are these?
How can you tell?

Answer: crocodiles

See and Compare

Alligator

Crocodile

tail
fringe on back legs
long, V-shaped snout
webbed feet
light olive or tan scales
teeth that always stick out

Quick Facts

Alligators and crocodiles are both reptiles. This means they are both cold-blooded and reproduce by laying eggs. Alligators and crocodiles are very similar. But they have some differences. Take a look!

Alligators

- live in fresh water
- can be up to 15 feet (4.6 meters) long
- do not have fringe on their back legs
- are not as aggressive as crocodiles

Crocodiles

- live in fresh and salt water
- can be up to 23 feet (7.0 meters) long
- have fringe on their back legs
- are more aggressive than alligators

Picture Glossary

fresh water
Water that does not have salt in it, such as the water in ponds.

fringe
A border on the edge of something.

salt water
Water that has salt in it, such as the water in oceans.

scales
Thin, flat, overlapping pieces of hard skin.

Index

To Learn More

Finding more information is as easy as 1, 2, 3.

1. Go to www.factsurfer.com
2. Enter "alligatororcrocodile?" into the search box.
3. Choose your book to see a list of websites.